C. 2

Monarchs

Stewart Ross

LUCENT BOOKS®

THOMSON
★
GALE™

San Diego • Detroit • New York • San Francisco • Cleveland • New Haven, Conn. • Waterville, Maine • London • Munich

THOMSON

GALE

Design: Peta Morey
Commissioning Editor: Jane Tyler
Editor: Liz Gogerly
Picture Researcher: Glass Onion Pictures
Consultant: Malcolm Barber
Map artwork: Encompass

We are grateful to the following for permission to reproduce photographs:
AKG, London 5, 6, 7, 10, 11, 12, 23, 30, 32, 33, 34, 41, 43; Art Archive (title), 14; Bridgeman Art Library/ Musee de la Tapisserie, Bayeux, France 4/ Musee Conde, Chantilly, France 9, 37/ Centre Historique des Archives Nationales, Paris, France 13/ Alecto Historical Editions, London, UK 15/ Arxiu de la Paeria, Lleida, Spain 16/ Victoria and Albert Museum, London, UK 18/ Private Collection 19/ Biblioteca Monasterio del Escorial, Madrid, Spain 22/ Bibliotheque Nationale, Paris, France 24, 28, 35, 38/ Peter Willi 25/ Louvre, Paris France 29/ British Library, London, UK 31, 40/ Lobkowicz Collections, Nelahozeves Castle, Czech Republic 39/ Chateau de Beauregard, France 44/ Barbar's Hall, London, UK 45; British Library 21 (top), 27; British Museum 42; Mary Evans 17; Stewart Ross 21 (bottom), 26.

Cover picture: © Gianni dagli Orti/CORBIS

Please note: Dates after monarchs refer to dates of reign unless otherwise noted.

LIBRARY OF CONGRESS CATALOGING-IN-PUBLICATION DATA

Ross, Stewart.
    Monarchs / by Stewart Ross.
        p. cm. — (Medieval realms)
Includes bibliographical references and index.
    ISBN 1-59018-535-8 (alk. paper)
    1.Kings and rulers—Biography. 2. Monarchy—Europe—History. 3. Europe—
Church history—600–1500. 4. Church and state—Europe—History. I. Title. II. Series

    D107.R66 2004
    940.1'092'2—dc22

                                                                2003060387

Contents

1066: The Year of the Three Kings

KING EDWARD of England (1042–1066), popularly known as Edward the Confessor, died on January 5, 1066. As it was not clear who should succeed him, Edward's rich and well-governed kingdom was a tempting prize for domestic and foreign adventurers ambitious for new land.

Whose Crown?

Three men put forward serious claims to the crown. King Harold Hadrada of Norway (1045–1066) said an old treaty made him King of England. **Duke** William of Normandy had a double claim: he was related to Edward and also claimed that the childless king had once named him as his successor.

The third contender, Earl Harold Godwinson, had the best claim. He was English, a proven leader, had been chosen by the Witan (a council of the important lords and bishops), and Edward had nominated him on his deathbed. Harold moved fast: the day after Edward's death he was formally made king at a religious ceremony in Westminster.

Wrong Message

Eleventh-century kings liked to be chosen by their powerful subjects. The Witan had chosen Harold, however, William had come to the crown by battle. At his coronation, therefore, he arranged for those present to be asked whether they accepted him. When they shouted that they did, the guards outside thought it was a riot and set fire to neighboring houses as a punishment!

The Bayeux Tapestry, a remarkable piece of linen needlework from the eleventh century, depicts the accession to the English throne of Duke William of Normandy. In this scene King Harold is shown holding the orb and scepter, symbols of his office, and is surrounded by Archbishop Stigand (right) and members of the nobility.

Trial by Battle

Neither Harold Hadrada nor Duke William were prepared to lose the crown without a fight, and they both began assembling invasion forces. To make things more difficult for Harold, his rebellious brother Tostig seemed prepared to help either Hadrada or William.

Tostig eventually sided with the Norwegians and, in late September, Harold Hadrada landed a large army on Tyneside. The new King of England went north with his elite troops, the **housecarls**, gathered reinforcements, and roundly defeated the invaders at the Battle of Stamford Bridge. Harold Hadrada and Tostig were both slain.

Harold's relief was cut short by news that Duke William had landed at Pevensey on the south coast. The king went swiftly south and arranged his army on Senlac Hill near Hastings. On October 14 William's forces, including many mounted knights, attacked fiercely and repeatedly, until they wore the English down. Some fled, but the king and his housecarls vainly fought on: By nightfall Harold lay dead and William was triumphant.

William the Conqueror (1066–1087) was crowned King of England in Westminster Abbey on Christmas Day 1066. The ceremony marked more than the **succession** of a new king— it was the beginning of a new chapter in the history of the English monarchy.

William the Conqueror (right) is portrayed defeating the Anglo Saxon king Harold II at the Battle of Hastings (1066) in this thirteenth-century manuscript.

The Anglo Saxon Chronicle, written by monks in 1066, recalls the Battle of Hastings:

"King Harold ... gathered together a great host, and came to oppose him [William] at the grey apple tree, and William came upon him unexpectedly.... Nevertheless the king fought against him most resolutely with those men who wished to stand beside him, and there was great slaughter on both sides. King Harold was slain, and Leofwine, his brother, and earl Gurth, his brother, and many good men. The French had possession of the place of slaughter, as God granted them...."

*The **Anglo Saxon** Chronicle*

The King and His Court

THE KING—ruler, lawgiver, judge, and army commander—was the very heart of his kingdom. No king could manage single-handedly, so the royal household was a curious mix of family, friends, servants, and **officers of state**. There were always others in attendance such as churchmen, **barons**, and representatives of other kings and dukes. Together they all made up the *curia regis* or king's court.

On the Move

The court was where the king was and, as few medieval monarchs were ever in one place for long, their court was peripatetic—it went around with them. Kings kept on the move for several reasons. It was a good way, in an age of poor communications, of keeping in touch with the kingdom. The word *court* reminds us that the royal court was also a law court (the highest in the land) where the king or his judges made decisions about many local cases.

The king's presence also reminded **subjects** of his glory—the kings of England and France claimed to be able to cure a skin disease called **scrofula** by touching the affected place. The court also moved around for practical reasons. Dozens of people living together put a huge strain on medieval sanitary arrangements. After a few weeks the court began, literally, to stink and had to find a fresher spot.

In this illustration of a manuscript by Jean Focquet (c. 1415–1477), John II of France and his wife Joanna, both wearing crowns, arrive at Paris after their coronation in 1350.

The King's Council

All kings needed advice. It was also wise for them to be seen to take advice: they could then claim that their decisions were made with the approval of others. Advice and approval came from the royal council, a gathering of leading figures in the realm—lay and church—whom the king chose to summon to discuss affairs of state.

Riot and Ceremony

The court lived off the region it was in. It was the locals' duty to provide for their lord, often for little or no payment, and supplies would soon run short. The court's arrival, therefore, might be a disaster, especially as **courtiers** could be rude, grasping, and riotous. Reportedly locals ran away and hid in the woods on hearing that the court of England's King John (1199–1216) was on its way to their area!

The court was a center of ceremony. Here, at least three times a year, the king appeared in public wearing his crown. To court flocked the leading writers, artists, and musicians. For example, Alfonso X of Spanish Castile (1252–1284) had dinner to the sound of singing and storytelling, while the court of France's John II (1350–1364) included the celebrated artist Girart d'Orléans.

(Right) Chronicler Jean de Froissart hands his manuscript to King Charles VI (1413–1422) of France. De Froissart's **Chronicles** *provides historians with important fourteenth-century evidence.*

(Below) England's Henry V (1380–1422) with his council. The king's early death in 1422 led to many turbulent years for his country.

Peter of Blois describes King Henry II of England (1154–1189):

"Although his legs are bruised and livid from hard riding, he never sits down except when on horseback or at meals.... He does not loiter in his palace like other kings, but hurrying through the provinces he investigates what is being done everywhere, and is especially strict in his judgement of those whom he has appointed judges of others."

The Medieval World, 300–1300

7

Royal Succession

AS SHOWN from the events in England in 1066, at the beginning of the Middle Ages there was no clear law on royal succession. Certain factors helped in a claim to the throne, including nomination by the previous monarch, blood relationship (but not necessarily being the eldest son), and election or approval by the ruling class. Ultimately, however, the surest way to come to the throne was simply to seize it.

Popular Choice

To begin with, all monarchs were to some extent elected—they could not rule without the support of the more powerful nobles.

The best example of an elected monarch was the **Holy Roman Emperor**. This title began in 800 when Pope Leo III made Charlemagne, King of the Franks (768–814), a new Roman Emperor. (The original Roman Empire had collapsed in the fifth century A.D.) The title became Holy in 1034 when Conrad II (King of Germany, 1024–1039) had a vast empire that included Germany, Austria, Switzerland,

A map shows the extent of the Holy Roman Empire in 1356.

The Holy Roman Empire
Holy Roman Empire c.1356
○ settlement

the Low Countries, Northern Italy, and parts of Eastern France and Eastern Europe.

In the twelfth century the Holy Roman Emperor—a powerful German ruler in his own right—was elected. At first many German princes voted. By the end of the next century, however, the number had been reduced to just seven: three archbishops (Mainz, Trier, and Cologne, now part of Germany) and the rulers of four states: the Palatinate, Brandenburg, Saxony (in modern Germany), and Bohemia (in the Czech Republic).

Hereditary Succession

Elsewhere the principle of **hereditary** succession was gradually accepted, the throne normally going to the eldest son of the previous king. France was the first major kingdom to accept this principle in law.

There were still problems, of course. These occurred when a monarch died childless, for instance, or when the law of succession was disputed. These occasions could lead to bitter and prolonged warfare, as in the Anglo-French Hundred Years War (see pages 34–35), Scotland's Wars of Independence (fought by the Scots to prevent their country from becoming absorbed into the Kingdom of England as Wales had been), and England's Wars of the Roses (see panel).

> **Wars of the Roses**
>
> The Wars of the Roses (1450–1487) were English civil wars in which the throne changed hands several times between two branches of the royal family. These were the Lancastrians (Henry VI and Henry VII), whose emblem was a red rose, and Yorkists (Edward IV, Richard III, and Edward V), whose emblem was a white rose. In fact, there were only about sixty weeks of fighting, and the causes of the long period of unrest were more complicated than just rivalry over the crown.

Charlemagne (right), in the time before the Holy Roman Emperor was elected, divided his kingdom between his three sons, Pepin, Charles, and Louis. The picture is from a fifteenth-century manuscript.

Coronations and Queens

THE WORD *king* had a special significance because of its religious associations. The Bible used it for God (King of Kings) and Jesus (King of the Jews). Many of the heroes of the Old Testament, like David and Solomon, were kings. So medieval kings were surrounded by a mystical, almost holy aura.

Coronation

A king's **coronation** emphasized his holiness. Coronations became more elaborate and important; indeed, before the ceremony a monarch was often called just ruler, not king.

A key part of the coronation was anointing the king with holy oil, making him a sort of priest. This gave him religious and **secular** status. The golden crown represented a form of halo. Once crowned, a king was under God's special protection. Some kings even claimed that as religious and secular lords they had power over both Church and state. As we shall see (see pages 24–25), disputes between kings and the Church were frequent and bitter.

Queens

A king's status as a semi-priest raised a huge problem for women rulers. As women were not admitted into the Church as priests, how could they be anointed as monarchs?

England's only female monarch, Matilda (lived 1102–1167, ruled 1135–1154) was never crowned. In neither France nor the kingdoms of Spain and Portugal did a woman rule until 1474, when Isabella became joint ruler of Castile, the largest Spanish kingdom, with her husband Ferdinand.

Henry I arranges for his daughter to succeed him:

1126: In this year King Henry held his court at Christmas in Windsor. David, the king of Scots, was present, and all the most important men in England, ecclesiastics [churchmen] and laymen; and there he obtained an oath from archbishops, bishops, abbots, earls, and all those thanes [lords] present, that England and Normandy should pass after his death into the possession of his daughter.

The Anglo Saxon Chronicle

Bishops pass the cup filled with holy oil for the anointing of Charles V (the Wise) of France in 1364. The ceremony took place at Reims, where all but six French monarchs were crowned.

10

Eleanor of Aquitaine

Although rarely ruling in their own right, women still had power and influence. Among the most remarkable queens was Eleanor, Duchess of Aquitaine (lived 1122–1204). She married two kings (Louis VII of France in 1137, and, in 1152, the future Henry II of England), and led troops on **crusade** and rebellions against her second husband.

While her son Richard I (the Lion Heart) of England (1189–1199) took part in the Second Crusade, she ruled as his **regent**. In 1200, aged seventy-eight, she put down a rebellion against another son, England's King John (1199–1216). Eleanor may have been exceptional, but her career shows that as wives, mothers, sisters, and lovers, medieval queens could play a vital part in medieval monarchy.

Eleanor of Aquitaine, the formidable heiress who married two kings and bore two others. She is depicted holding a religious book to indicate her learning and piety.

Margaret of Anjou (lived 1429–1482)

Owing to her feeble husband's mental illness, for long periods the formidable French queen of England's Henry VI virtually took over his role as sovereign. During the Wars of the Roses (see page 9) Margaret championed his cause until defeated and captured in 1471. She was then held in the Tower of London for four years until **ransomed** by France's Louis XI (1461–1483) and allowed to return home to France.

Royal Government

A KING was expected to govern his kingdom upholding law and order so his subjects could live in peace and security. In practice, a great deal of government was not in his hands at all but took place at a more local level. Each lord, for example, held his own law court. Worried that he had little control over local matters, France's Philip II (1180–1223) took the unusual step of setting up a system of paid royal servants (bailiffs) to keep an eye on local affairs.

The Household

Originally royal government was carried out by the king's household. In time, however, as government became more complicated, household departments grew into departments of state. A good example of this was the wardrobe in England. State departments like the wardrobe did not travel around with the monarch but set up permanent offices operating from the same place.

Originally, as its name implies, the wardrobe was responsible for royal clothing, armor, and so forth. Henry III (1216–1272) and Edward I (1272–1307) adapted the wardrobe into a government office responsible for war funds.

France's Louis XI (1461–1483) with knights of the Order of St. Michael. Such displays of magnificence show how he was eager to outdo the chivalric glory of the household of his neighbor and rival, Duke Charles of Burgundy (1467–1477).

Illiterate Masters

Most early medieval monarchs were illiterate. In fact, Henry I (1100–1135) was the first English king after the Norman Conquest who could read and write. Two important results followed. First, kings needed reliable servants who were literate. These clerks (secretaries) were normally churchmen as the Church ran virtually all formal education. The king's chief secretary was the chancellor, whose office was the **chancery**. In time the English chancery developed into a law court.

The second effect of the king's illiteracy was the use of seals. These were picture impressions made on soft wax (or sometimes lead) and attached to a document to prove it was genuine. (An illiterate king, of course, could not add his signature. Even if he could, those receiving the document might themselves be illiterate.)

The chancellor kept the Great Seal, which was used for documents of great importance (such as the Magna Carta, see page 19). A smaller Privy Seal was used for everyday matters and documents of less importance.

see page 19

The Wonder of the World

So many and great were the talents of Holy Roman Emperor Frederick II (1212–1250) that he was known as the Wonder of the World. He was not just an able warrior and politician but also a scholar of some note. At a time when most monarchs were still semi-literate, he spoke many languages and wrote poetry in Italian and a book in Latin on hunting.

Literacy was rare in England so Henry II (1154–1189) ordered his **justices** to read out this Assize [instruction] in every county, to make sure that everybody knew about it:

"Every knight shall possess a coat of mail, helmet, shield and lance.... Also, every free layman who is worth 16 marks in goods or rents shall possess a hauberk, helmet, shield and lance. Also, every free layman who is worth 10 marks in goods or rents shall possess a mail shirt, iron headpiece and lance. Also, all townspeople and freemen shall possess a quilted tunic, iron headpiece and lance."

A Documentary History of England

The Great Seal of Henry II of England shows the king on horseback in full fighting armor.

Royal Finance

KINGS NEEDED money. They needed it for personal requirements, such as clothes, jewels, horses, and hunting dogs, and also for government. By far their biggest item of expenditure was war. A successful campaign, however, could bring huge profits in captured lands, loot, and ransoms. The ransom demanded for King John II of France (1350–1364), captured by the Black Prince (the eldest son of England's Edward III, 1327–1377) at the Battle of Poitiers (1356), was £500,000 (about $750,000 today)—several times the King of England's normal annual income and far more than the prince had spent on his campaign.

Royal Income

Apart from possible profits of war, kings had four main sources of income. The most reliable one was their own personal lands, which provided rents and goods like wood, wine, and meat.

The king was the highest lord in the land (see pages 18–19). Lesser lords (his **vassals**) had to pay for certain rights and permissions. A vassal paid the king a relief, for example, in order to inherit his father's estates. Monarchs also claimed an aid to help pay for the marriage of their sons and daughters.

It was the duty of the king's vassals to provide military service in time of war. By the late thirteenth century it

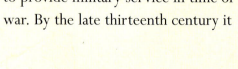

A fifteenth-century French manuscript illustration shows subjects bringing tax in the form of gold to a grateful-looking king.

Cities

Medieval economic expansion made monarchs richer and allowed them to employ **mercenaries** and more paid officials. However, it also gave rise to great cities like Paris, London, Toledo, Cologne, and Milan that by late-medieval times were almost as rich and powerful as any monarch. Needing the cities' loans and money from taxation, monarchs were eager to keep on good terms with them.

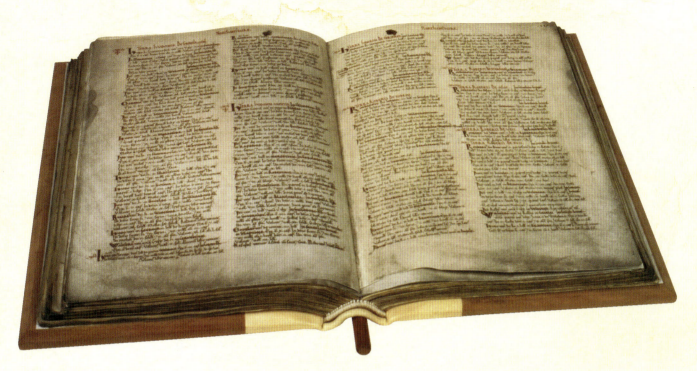

England's greatest book—the Domesday Book—*was William the Conqueror's comprehensive survey of his kingdom.*

was usual for kings to receive payment (shield money or scutage) rather than actual service. The scutage might then be used to hire mercenaries or to pay volunteers, both of whom were more reliable than unwilling vassals.

Taxes

The monies mentioned above were rarely sufficient to meet all a king's needs. To fill the gaps, kings turned to taxation. A few taxes, like customs (payable on goods entering the country) and on vital items like salt, were regular. Most, however, were collected only to meet emergencies. These included poll taxes (head taxes payable by everyone) and taxes on land and on moveable possessions like cows and sheep. Henry II (1154–1189) first raised a tax on moveables and incomes in England in 1166.

Taxes that did not distinguish between rich and poor were particularly unpopular. These included the French salt tax (the *gabelle*) and the English poll tax that sparked the **Peasants' Revolt** of 1381. As tax collection was difficult and unpopular, some monarchs sold the task to favored individuals (tax farmers) who kept any profits they made.

The *Domesday Book,* 1086–1087

To know who owned what and how much service and rent was due to him, William the Conqueror (1066–1087) arranged for a massive survey of his kingdom. It was so detailed, listing not just manors but cows and sheep, that his English subjects said it was like Do(o)mesday—the Day of Judgment mentioned in the Bible.

Monarchs and Representatives

KINGS CLAIMED, rightly or wrongly, that they ruled with the consent of their people. Moreover, a wise king always made sure that he kept in touch with his subjects and at least made a show of consulting with the more important ones before making a major decision. Different bodies developed from this consultation process. These were known as estates, cortes, diets, and parliaments.

Estates, Cortes, and Diets

The French Estates General, first summoned in 1302 by Philip IV (1285–1314), was an assembly of representatives to help the king. It consisted of members of the three estates (groups of people) of the realm: the **clergy**, **nobility,** and **common people**. They did not work well together and met infrequently and reluctantly.

In the kingdoms of the Iberian Peninsula (Castile, Leon, Catalonia, Valencia, Navarre, Portugal) meetings of the estates were known as cortes. In Castile, the **Third Estate** was made up of

These instructions about how to hold a parliament in 1320 still apply in the British parliament today:

"All members of Parliament will sit and no one will stand except to speak. Members should speak so as to be heard by everyone in Parliament. No one will enter or leave Parliament, except by the one door. A member will stand to say anything which should be debated by Parliament."

A Documentary History of England

James the Just of Aragon with the parliament (cortes) that met in Barcelona in 1311. The formidable royal presence made even the thought of free speech almost impossible.

representatives from the towns that the monarch relied on for funding.

From 1100 onward the Holy Roman Emperors summoned meetings of the German nobility, higher clergy, barons, knights, and, later, representatives, from the major cities to discuss new laws. These meetings were called diets and they met in whichever city the emperor chose. Unusually, by the later Middle Ages, the power of the diets was increasing as that of the emperors declined.

Parliament

In the long run, the most significant of these representative bodies was the English parliament.
It began as a meeting of the nobles and bishops of the king's Great Council. In the thirteenth century, two representatives of each shire (county) and of each major borough (town) were told to meet with the council. These meetings became known as a parliament.

In time, the shire and borough representatives met in a House of Commons, separate from the nobles and bishops who met in a House of Lords. Originally summoned to give support and advice, parliaments gradually became more powerful. New laws (statutes) needed the approval of both king and parliament, and monarchs also required parliament's approval to raise new taxes. Even so, a parliament did not meet unless summoned by the monarch.

Scotland's Parliament

The first mention of a Scottish parliament is in July 1290. It meant a formal meeting of the king and his counselors: 12 bishops, 23 abbots, 11 **priors**, 12 earls, and 50 barons. Before long, as in England, Scottish parliaments came to include representatives of the common people too.

An Ordered Society

MOST EUROPEANS felt they belonged to a particular rank or layer in society. This organization (sometimes known as feudalism) lasted in much of Europe until about 1300, although it lingered on in some places, such as Hungary, until the twentieth century. Essentially, society was a network of responsibility between the three estates of clergy, nobility, and common people (see page 16). Kings were at the hub of this network.

Fiefs

Society was based on land, which was the main source of wealth. The theory said that God had given the emperor and kings responsibility for all nonspiritual matters. This meant that all land was theoretically theirs, and they controlled all legal matters. Indeed, French kings claimed that they were the source of all legal power.

Kings handed out large parcels of land (fiefs) to their vassals, sometimes also known as tenants-in-chief. These vassals—the great nobles of the realm—owed the king military service and advice. In return, the king offered them justice, protection, and education for their sons.

This organization was clearer in

Work in return for land and protection: a fifteenth-century depiction of peasants working for their lord. The man in the foreground is plowing with oxen.

England than elsewhere because the events of 1066 gave William the Conqueror (1066–1087) the chance to start with a clean slate, handing out land to those who had supported him. Nevertheless, he was careful not to give anyone enough land in a single region for them to become a petty king there.

Fealty and Honor

The large fiefs were subdivided. The nobles had vassals of their own, on much the same terms as their relationship with the king. Within the Church, this meant that a monastery that had received land from the king, for example, might well act as a lord and have vassals of its own.

At the bottom of society were the ordinary peasants, who worked their lord's land and did other labor such as carpentry. They also had use of **common land** on which they could graze their livestock. Their lord had the duty to hear their cases in his court and protect them against evil-doers.

Society paid much attention to the ideas of honor and duty. The relationship between lord and vassal was cemented by an oath (called an act of homage) in which the latter swore fealty (faithful service). If a lord, even a king, failed to stick to his part of the bargain, vassals were entitled to feel aggrieved. This lay at the heart of the dispute that produced the Magna Carta (see panel).

The Magna Carta, 1215

The Magna Carta was a document signed by King John of England (1199–1216), following a rebellion by barons, in which he promised to follow his duty and uphold good government, by the law of the land. Other kings had issued such charters, so at the time John's was not remarkable. From the seventeenth century, however, the event was regarded as the cornerstone of the rights of English and American people.

A Victorian engraving of the signing of the Magna Carta. The Great Charter was one of several similar medieval documents which became famous when it was rediscovered in the seventeenth century.

Keeping Control

CONTROLLING MORE distant parts of the realm was a tricky business. Although vassals swore to honor and obey their lord, there were always some whose loyalty could not be trusted. England's Henry II (1154–1189) even faced rebellion from his own sons, backed by their mother, Eleanor of Aquitaine (see page 11).

Slow communications made the problem more difficult—a message traveled no faster than the speed of a horse. Moreover, kings could not afford to keep an army always at the ready. Forces were gathered for each fresh occasion they were needed.

Scattered Honors

A vassal's lands were known as his honor. So lords did not build up a strong regional power base, monarchs tried to keep honors scattered around the kingdom. The best opportunity for this came to William I (1066–1087) after his conquest of England: the honor he gave to his follower William FitzAnsculf, for example, was spread around a dozen counties.

However, frontier regions (known as marches) needed powerful lords to protect the kingdom from outside attack. The tactic here was to use families who were wholly dependent on the monarch for their advancement. Such people were less likely to rebel. Henry I of England (1100–1135), for instance, gave key lands in Shropshire, on the Welsh marches, to the relatively unknown FitzAlan family from Brittany.

Royal Strongholds

Effective monarchs were always on the move. Since they could not be everywhere at once, they also established powerful symbols of their authority in strategic places. These symbols were royal castles.

The French bishop Fulbert of Chartres outlines the duties of a vassal to his lord:

"He who swears fealty [loyalty] to his lord ought always to have these six things in his memory: what is harmless, safe, honourable, useful, easy, practicable."

The Medieval World 300–1300

Gunpowder

The invention of the cannon in the fourteenth century was a great blow to royal authority. Royal castles could now be battered into submission in days. However, as usually only monarchs could afford large guns, they were more used by kings than against them—Scotland's James II (1437–1460) even blew himself up by taking too close an interest in his beloved cannon.

One of the first acts of William I after his coronation was the building of a castle in London. This was later developed into the famous Tower of London, built 1078–1097 and strengthened by later generations. It served as a royal fortress, palace, prison, and, by the time of Henry III (1216–1272), zoo.

The castle of Richard I of England (1189–1199) at Château Gaillard is perhaps the most famous example of such a royal stronghold. Perched on a rock overlooking the River Seine at Les Andelys, Normandy, it reminded all who looked on it of the might of Richard the Lion Heart. Its fall in 1204, during the reign of Richard's brother John (1199–1216), marked the end of his power in the region.

(Right) A depiction of medieval London dominated by the Tower of London. The old London Bridge, with houses and shops on it, is shown in the background.

(Below) The great fortress of Château Gaillard in France. During the siege of 1204 it fell because troops of Philip II of France (1179–1223) found a way in through a toilet shaft.

The King and the Law

KINGS SWORE at their coronation to uphold the law. But what was the law? In the early Middle Ages no European country had an organized legal system. The law was a mix of ancient custom, barons' decisions, and royal order.

To complicate matters further, the Church had its own network of law and courts (see pages 26–27). One of the great achievements of medieval government was to clean up this mess and set up systems that are the basis of our law today.

The Law of Justinian

The development of organized law occurred in two very different ways. One took place in most of continental Europe, the other in England. The two were—and remain— fundamentally different.

Eleventh-century scholars working in northern Italy rediscovered a code of law drawn up by the Roman Emperor Justinian I (527–565) in the eastern Roman capital of

A fourteenth-century manuscript shows a king dispensing justice to kneeling subjects. A monarch wielding such power is difficult for us to imagine—the nearest modern equivalent would be a dictator.

Medieval monarchs approved of the code's emphasis on royal authority as seen in this excerpt from the Justinian Code:

"After having concluded this work [sorting out the law] and collected it all in a single volume under our Illustrious name.... We have hastened to attempt the most complete and thorough amendment of the entire law.... Therefore We order that everything shall be governed by these ... works."

The Medieval World 300–1300

Constantinople. This *Corpus Juris Civilis* (Code of Civil Law) swiftly spread around the continent. The Emperor Barbarossa took it on in the 1160s and the French kings shortly afterward. It provided a clear set of laws with the king at its center. The code, for instance, declared that the king was emperor in his own kingdom.

Because the Justinian Code was written down, it had to be studied to be understood. Law schools, such as the one at Montpellier in France, were set up. Men trained in the law developed clear, logical minds and made excellent royal servants.

The English Experience

For reasons of cost and convenience, the kings of England did not adopt the Justinian Code. They tidied up the existing system of local and royal courts, keeping the principle that justice came from the people. This meant the survival of the **Anglo Saxon** jury system, still used in Britain and the United States.

English law was based on custom, previous court judgments, and acts (new laws) agreed to by the king and his parliament. The system was watched over by royal justices traveling around to local courts.

Off with his head! Louis XI (1461–1483) of France decrees the death sentence for Charles de Melun, Lord of Normanville, in 1468. Louis held a grudge against the man, who was not guilty of the treason of which he had actually been accused.

Trial by Ordeal

Ordeal was a kind of test of guilt or innocence in which the judgment was made by God. In ordeal by hot iron the accused carried a red-hot iron for a number of paces then had his or her hand bound up. It was inspected three days later: satisfactory healing was a God-given sign of innocence. This barbaric practice was little used after the early thirteenth century. Trial by water involved the accused being thrown into a pool: if they sank, they were innocent!

Kings and the Church

MEDIEVAL **CHRISTENDOM** was deeply religious. This did not just mean people went to church. God was believed to be active in everything. Ill fortune was seen as punishment for wrongdoing.

The Church taught that priests were the link between man and God. A priest praying for the soul of a dead person hastened its journey to heaven. Not surprisingly, the Church was showered with gifts and money, making it very wealthy. Moreover, for much of the Middle Ages, the Church had almost total control of formal education.

Cooperation and Conflict

Wealth gave the Church great power, and it was in rulers' interests to work with it. A good example was the Crusades, launched by Pope Urban II in 1095. After a slow start, rulers threw themselves with great energy into the Church's campaign to capture the Holy Land from the Muslims (see page 28).

Nevertheless, conflict between Church and state was inevitable. One area of friction was the appointment of bishops and archbishops, known as the investiture dispute. As they controlled rich and widespread estates, kings wanted a say in who held such posts. The popes said it was none of their business.

An eighteenth-century engraving of Emperor Henry IV at the feet of Pope Gregory VII in the late eleventh century. The struggle between monarchs and the Church was a constant feature of medieval politics.

The Great Schism

By bringing great shame to the Church, the Great Schism helped monarchs tighten control over it in their kingdoms. The problem began with the election of Pope Urban VI in 1378, which was disputed by the French. They elected a rival, Clement VIII, who was set up in Avignon, France. The dispute continued, at one stage producing three popes at the same time, until all sides agreed to accept Martin V in 1417.

Pope Urban II writes to the Spanish King Alfonso VI (1065–1109), reminding him that spiritual was greater than **secular** power:

"There are two powers, O King, which mainly rule the world: priestly dignity and royal authority. But priestly dignity, my very dear son, so very much surpasses royal authority because we have to account to the king of the universe [God] for the acts of kings themselves."

Europe: A History of Its Peoples

The imposing west front of Notre Dame Cathedral, Amiens, France, remains a symbol of the power and majesty of God and his Church on Earth. Such buildings were more impressive than anything in the king's possession.

The pope generally came out on top in investiture disputes. In 1207, for instance, King John of England (1199–1216) refused to accept Pope Innocent III's appointment of Stephen Langton as Archbishop of Canterbury. The pope retaliated by placing England under an **interdict**. This meant no church services, not even marriages or burials, were allowed until the king backed down in 1213.

Pope and Emperor

The most spectacular Church versus state battle came in the time of Holy Roman Emperor Henry IV (1056–1106). In 1076, after Pope Gregory VII had interfered in German affairs, the emperor said he was no longer pope. Gregory then **excommunicated** Henry, cutting him off from the Church.

Emperor and pope made peace and argued several times. Henry even besieged Rome and made a second pope, Clement III, who recrowned him. The conflict rumbled on until 1122, by which time both Henry and Gregory were dead.

Henry II and Thomas Becket

CHURCH COURTS tried those who had broken church law on matters such as immorality. They also heard cases involving churchmen or clerks. The definition of a clerk was elastic, allowing all kinds of people (including obvious frauds) to claim this benefit of the clergy. The problem for monarchs who wanted to clamp down on criminal behavior was that Church courts were more lenient than civil courts. They had, for example, no death penalty.

The Constitutions of Clarendon

In 1164, Henry II summoned a council to meet at Clarendon, Wiltshire. There he set out what he saw as his traditional rights over the English Church. At first Thomas Becket accepted these Constitutions of Clarendon, which seemed to undermine the benefit of the clergy. Later, he regretted his decision, a move that infuriated the king.

The King's Friend

Henry II (1154–1189), a vigorous and intelligent king, was determined to take action against the lawlessness that was widespread throughout his English kingdom. On many occasions, however, he found that criminals claimed benefit of clergy (criminous clerks) and got off lightly at their trials in Church courts.

In 1162, on the death of Archbishop Theobald of Canterbury, Henry saw a chance to tighten his grip over the Church and its criminous clerks. He persuaded his friend and chancellor, Thomas Becket, to become the next archbishop. Becket was made a priest and the next day the reluctant monks of Canterbury elected him archbishop.

Canterbury Cathedral as it looks today. Thomas Becket is depicted in stained glass in the cathedral.

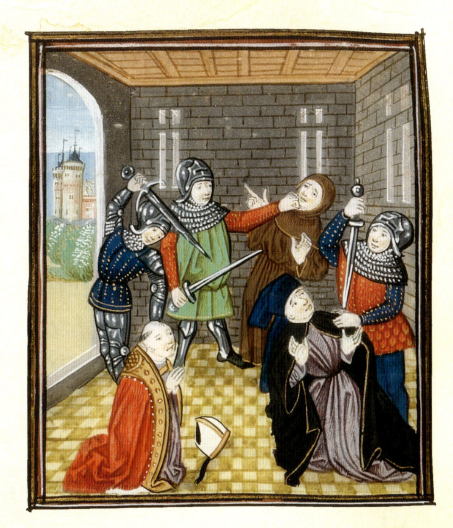

Sacrilege! Four knights assault the monks of Canterbury Cathedral before turning on Archbishop Thomas Becket (kneeling left).

The Turbulent Priest

To Henry's intense irritation, Becket now took the Church's side in all disputes with the king, including the question of criminous clerks. In 1164 the king brought Becket himself to trial. Knowing how ruthless his former master could be, Becket fled to France and remained there for almost six years. King Louis VII of France (1137–1180) and the pope tried in vain to mediate.

Becket returned to England in 1170 and excommunicated the Archbishop of York and two other bishops for bending to the king's will. The move was clearly provocative. At his Christmas court in Normandy, Henry lost his temper and wondered out loud whether anyone would rid him of the turbulent priest.

Four knights took the king at his word. They crossed to England, found Becket in Canterbury Cathedral, and brutally hacked him to death on the steps of the high altar. Christendom was horror-struck. While Henry allowed himself to be publicly flogged, his former friend was declared a saint.

In retelling the story of the murder, monks gave Thomas Becket a Christ-like saintliness:

"Next he received a second blow on the head, but still he stood firm and immovable. At the third blow he fell on his knees and elbows, offering himself [as] a living sacrifice and saying in a low voice, 'For the name of Jesus and the protection of the Church I am ready to embrace death.' But the third knight inflicted a terrible wound ... and the crown of his head ... was separated from the head."

The High Middle Ages, 1000–1300

Crusading Kings

TO MEDIEVAL KINGS, war was almost a sport. It was not an activity to be avoided but one to be practiced for and participated in, when it came, with pride and enthusiasm. The call of Pope Urban II for a crusade against the Muslim infidel (see page 24), therefore, should have inspired monarchs to take up the Christian sword immediately. In fact, not one king came forward to lead the First Crusade (1095–1099).

Politics and Faith

Urban had recently excommunicated the Holy Roman Emperor and King Philip I of France (1060–1108), making them ineligible to lead the mission. England's William II (1087–1100), unsure that he supported Urban in his squabble with the emperor, also declined. Despite not having a king to lead them, the crusading knights conquered a narrow strip of land at the eastern end of the Mediterranean.

By the time of the Second Crusade (1147–1149) the pope and European monarchs were on better terms. The Holy Roman Emperor, Conrad III (1138–1152) and Louis VIII of France (1137–1180) raised armies for the Holy Land, but they did not get along with each other or with the Christian rulers of the region. Consequently, their campaign achieved little and was abandoned after a fruitless attack on Damascus.

Taking Advantage

The church threatened dire punishment on anyone who touched a crusader's possessions while he was away. Nevertheless, rulers often left home at their own cost. When Duke Robert of Normandy was on the First Crusade he lost the opportunity to become King of England. In his absence, in 1100 the crown was seized by Henry (Henry I), his younger brother, who later took Normandy as well.

A fourteenth-century illustration of knights on crusade. Note that they bear their own emblems of chivalry, not the red cross on a white background that is shown in many modern pictures.

Later Crusaders

The Third Crusade (1189–1192) attracted no less than three monarchs: the Holy Roman Emperor Frederick Barbarossa (1152–1190), Philip II of France (1180–1223), and Richard I of England (1189–1199). They worked together slightly better than their royal predecessors but with limited success. Barbarossa drowned before reaching the Holy Land. Philip argued with his English neighbor and came back early. Richard was captured on the way home (see page 31), and Jerusalem remained in Muslim hands.

The most famous of the later crusader kings was France's Louis IX (1226–1270), who became known as Saint Louis. During a severe illness he promised to go on a crusade, and on his recovery he duly set out on the Sixth Crusade (1248–1254). Saint he might have been, but soldier he was not. He was defeated, captured, and had to be ransomed by his people.

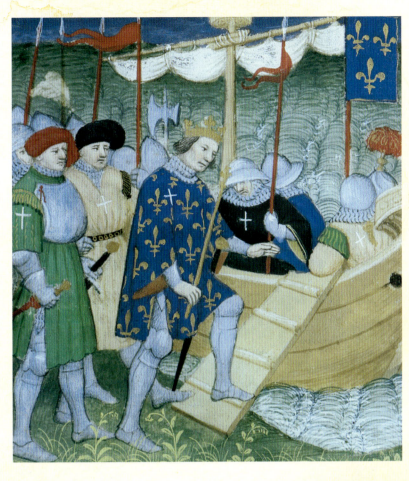

France's Saint Louis sets off for the Holy Land. The venture proved very expensive as the king was captured and freed only after an enormous ransom had been paid.

John, Lord of Joinville, recalls Louis IX of France taking the cross—pledging to go on a crusade:

"King Louis … was taken very seriously ill, and came so near to dying that one of the two ladies who were tending him wanted to draw the sheet over his face. But another lady … said she was sure his soul was still in his body. As the king lay listening to the dispute … our Lord worked within him and … as soon as he was able to speak he asked for the cross to be given him; and this was promptly done."
Chronicles of the Crusades

The Chivalrous Crusader

FROM THE late twelfth century onward a monarch was expected to be chivalrous. **Chivalry** was an unwritten code of behavior, inspired by the Church, that tried to take the rough edges off knights who lived to fight.

A chivalrous knight had to be courageous, of course. Off the battlefield he was supposed to be less brutal, protecting the weak (especially women), giving gifts freely, behaving with courtesy, and always being loyal to friends and his lord. After a victorious fight he should show mercy to defeated enemies, particularly if they were of the same class as himself.

Richard the Lion Heart

Richard I of England (1189–1199), a legend in his own lifetime, was one of the earliest kings to be hailed as a model of chivalry.

Berengaria (died 1230)

Richard married Berengaria of Navarre (in Spain) in Cyprus in 1191. The new Queen of England never once set foot in that country and hardly saw her husband after 1194. They had no children. In truth, the marriage was just a way of making sure that her father, King Sancho VI of Navarre (1150–1194), did not attack Richard's French territories during his absence.

A fifteenth-century illustration of the siege of Damascus in the Second Crusade (1148). The artist uses a European landscape and the costume and weaponry of his own era.

Richard left for the Holy Land in 1190, shortly after his coronation as King of England. He captured Cyprus, was present when the Christians retook the great fortress of Acre in 1191, and defeated the mighty Muslim leader Saladin (lived 1138–1193) at the Battle of Arsuf in the Holy Land.

Not powerful enough to take Jerusalem, he negotiated terms with Saladin. The agreement allowed Christian **pilgrims** to visit the holy city. On his way home Richard was captured by the Duke of Austria and not released until 1194 on payment of a ransom of 100,000 marks. He spent most of the rest of his reign retaking lands that France's Philip II (1179–1223) had captured in his absence.

The New Arthur

The Lion Heart probably deserves his reputation. He was a fine warrior and respected his enemies: while in the Holy Land he exchanged gifts and had long and amicable discussions with Saladin and his brother. In his absence, his European territories were on the whole well governed.

Richard did not leave his reputation to chance, however. An intelligent and well-educated man, a songwriter and good with words, he deliberately built up the picture of himself as the new King Arthur. In a sense this was all very modern—the deliberate creation of the image of a chivalrous celebrity.

Richard writes home about his exploits in the Crusades:

"Within a short period of our arrival and that of the French king we had regained Acre…. However, the French king left us after fifteen days and returned to his own country. We, on the other hand, are more concerned with the love and honour due to God than an audacious [daring] interest in the acquisition [seizing] … of territories."
Chronicles of the Crusades

Mutual respect—a fourteenth-century picture of England's crusader King Richard I jousting with his enemy, Saladin, the Turkish leader. The artist, himself a Christian, depicts the Christian coming off best.

Kings at War

WARFARE WAS AT the heart of early medieval society. Every able-bodied man was expected to bear arms if his king called upon him to do so. Kings, as long as they could stay in the saddle, were expected to lead their men into battle. Edward I of England (1272–1307) was sixty-eight when he last took an army north to fight the Scots. His contemporary, France's Saint Louis (1226–1270), was one of the few monarchs whose reputation did not rest on his military ability (see page 29).

Raising an Army

In theory, a king could ask his vassals to provide an army whenever he needed one. This was never as easy as it sounded, and the quality of such an army was dubious. The locals who fought with Harold at Hastings, for example, were no match for William's armored knights on horseback. In one sense, though, Harold was lucky—at least his army showed up. Later levies, as they were called, had a reputation for being slow to come forward and swift to desert. In response, monarchs came to rely more on paid troops, some of them professional soldiers.

The Bruce and Bannockburn

The victory of Scotland's Robert I (the Bruce, 1306–1329) over England's Edward II (1307–1327) at Bannockburn in 1314 was one of the more important medieval battles. Knowing defeat would probably finish him, Bruce was reluctant to give battle. When he finally did so, however, the incompetent English commanders played into his hands and his total victory secured his kingdom's independence for many years.

The death of Harold at the Battle of Hastings, 1066. The victory of Duke William of Normandy was partly due to his use of the latest weapons and armored knights mounted on horseback.

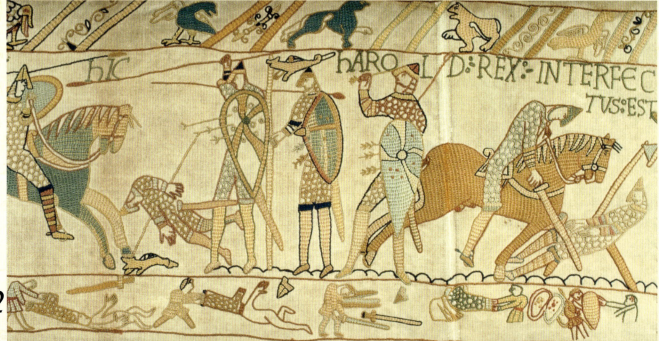

A battle that shaped the map of Europe: the forces of King John of Portugal overcome those of his Spanish neighbor, King John of Castile, at the battle of Aljubarrota in 1385.

The Cost of War

Warfare became steadily more and more expensive, and not just because wages had to be paid. Sophisticated weapons, from **siege engines** to large crossbows and brass cannons, were also very costly.

High spending meant high taxes, and high taxes meant a discontented people. It is no coincidence that two massive peasants' revolts, in France (1358) and England (1381), occurred when taxes were rising to pay for the Hundred Years War (see pages 34–35).

As troops were expensive and defeat often catastrophic, kings avoided large-scale battles. They preferred wasting, devastating their enemy's territory and taking all the loot they could find. This kept the troops happy and helped pay for the campaign. Nevertheless, the impact of a great victory, such as the Portuguese triumph over Castile at Aljubarrota on the Iberian Peninsula in 1385, might last for decades, even centuries.

Although in middle age France's Louis VI (1108–1137) was so fat he could not get on his horse, in his youth he displayed vigorous bravery:

"Impatient of delay, the Lord Louis, consumed one day by energy, summoned the army, and approached that castle which was brilliantly defended by a deep and steep ditch topped by a wall, and below by a rushing stream whose depth made it virtually impregnable. The Lord Louis crossed the stream, scaled the earthwork with its barrier, came up to the wall, gave the order for battle while fighting himself, and led an attack on the enemy as violent as it was bitter."

Life of King Louis the Fat

One Hundred Years of War

THE HUNDRED YEARS WAR was really a series of conflicts that happened over 115 years (1338–1453). The stage was mostly France and the cast largely the French and English kings and their subjects. From time to time, however, Burgundians, Scots, Spanish, and others became involved.

Opposing Claims

Medieval people thought of themselves as belonging to Christendom and their local lord, not their nation. It was not strange for England and parts of France to be under a single ruler after 1066, and barons commonly held lands on both sides of the English Channel. The idea of **nationalism** emerged only in the later Middle Ages (see pages 36–37).

A monarch was expected to expand his territories where possible, even through war. Philip of Valois (Philip VI, 1328–1350) claimed the French throne as the son of the younger brother of Philip the Fair (1285–1324). However, Edward III of England (1327–1377), of the Plantaganet family, said he had a better claim through his mother Isabella, the daughter of Philip the Fair. This, together with the attempts by the French to wrest control of Gascony, brought Edward and Philip to war in 1338.

Changing Warfare

At first the conflict was between the Plantaganet and Valois dynasties rather than between England and France. But by the time it ended, especially after Joan of Arc (1412–1431) had rallied French spirits, it was beginning to look more like a modern war between two nations.

At the age of 13, Joan of Arc claimed she heard voices telling her to rescue the French from the English. She briefly inspired her people to rise up and fight, before being captured and executed by the English. She is now the patron saint of France.

34

France, richer and larger than England, had to focus all its resources for victory. It also needed to bring the way it waged war up to date. The English victory at Crécy (1346) marked the end of the supremacy of the mounted knights so beloved of the French kings. At Poitiers (1356) and Agincourt (1415) they were again brought down by longbow archers. What the bow started, the **pike** and cannon then finished, and the massed charge of mounted knights in armor became a thing of the past.

When, in the later 1420s, the full wealth and might of the French crown was eventually brought to bear, England's possessions in France were doomed. By 1453, the only ones left in English hands were Calais and the Channel Islands. Kings of England continued to call themselves kings of France, but it was now just an honorary title. United under powerful modernizing monarchs, France was no longer an easy prey to the English.

A fifteenth-century picture of Crécy depicts one of the battles that marked the beginning of the end of the supremacy of the mounted knight on the battlefield.

The French chronicler, Jean de Froissart reports the opening shots at the Battle of Crécy:

"Then the English archers stepped forth one pace and let fly their arrows so wholly and so thick that it seemed snow. When the Genoese [mercenaries] felt the arrows piercing through heads, arms and breasts, many of them cast down their crossbows and did cut their strings and returned discomforted. When the French king saw them fly away he said, 'Slay the rascals!'"

Renaissance and Reformation 1300–1648

Henry the Hero

Henry V (1413–1422) exploited French weaknesses by reopening the Hundred Years War in 1415. His dramatic victory at Agincourt made him a national hero. He went on to conquer all Normandy and become heir to the French throne. His use of English as the language of administration in his new possessions shows how the war was becoming more nationalistic.

35

The Birth of Nations

BY THE LATER Middle Ages monarchs were generally more powerful than they had been in the eleventh century. Some developments, such as estates and parliaments, limited their authority. Nevertheless, Church decline, more centralized law, improved government, and possession of cannons all added to their power (see pages 16–17).

Logical Kingdoms

Eleventh-century Europe was a patchwork of kingdoms, cities, counties, and other territories. Spain, for example, was half in Muslim Arab hands and half divided between the Christian territories of Castile, Portugal, Navarre, Aragon, and Catalonia as they were then, in the Iberian Peninsula. The exception was

This map shows how Europe was divided in about 1500.

Founders of modern Spain: King Ferdinand of Aragon and Queen Isabella of Castile with their daughter, Joanna. Their remarkable reign saw the reconquest of the Muslim south of the country and the establishment of the Spanish Empire in the New World.

the Holy Roman Empire, but this was more a collection of semi-independent states than an actual realm governed by a single person.

One of the chief developments of the medieval period was the forging of some realms into modern-looking states. In 1266, Alexander III (1249–1286) expanded his rule to include all Scotland. Modern Spain came into being with the marriage of King Ferdinand of Aragon (1479–1516) and Isabella of Castile (1474–1504) in 1469. Adopting the title tsar in 1472, Ivan the Great took an important step toward creating the Kingdom of Russia. The principal exceptions were Germany and Italy. They remained divided between smaller kingdoms, states, and cities until the nineteenth century.

Majesty

Early medieval kings were lords of their lands, but many were rough and ready warriors, illiterate and ignorant of the subtleties of law and administration. However, as their kingdoms expanded and were united by tighter government, emphasis was placed on the head of state. By the end of the fifteenth century a monarch was developing into something more than a lord—he was emerging as a living representative of his nation.

This change involved monarchs becoming more distant and majestic. They were better educated and their coronations and courts more splendid. By spending more time in their private accommodation, their public appearances were more special. Forms of address—use of Your Majesty rather than just Sire—reflected this growing royal prestige.

The Scottish Nation

Scotland was one of the earliest European countries to discover a sense of nationhood based around its king. An important influence was the fight to prevent the kings of England, notably Edward I, from taking over the country after 1296. Successive kings, starting with Robert the Bruce, put themselves at the head of the nation's struggle that continued until well into the fourteenth century.

Royal Successes

TO RULE EFFECTIVELY, monarchs needed to be soldiers, lawyers, and administrators rolled into one. They also required physical strength and stamina, almost superhuman energy, and a sharp understanding of human nature. It helped to be seen as holy, too.

Too often twisted by flattery and power, monarchs were rarely pleasant people, although most could be charming if the need arose. Those who contributed most were, for the most part, ruthless, even cruel in their ambition.

The Warriors

The great majority of warrior kings—such as William the Conqueror (1066–1087), Louis VIII (the Lion, 1223–1226), England's Edward I (1272–1307), Ivan the Great of Russia (1462–1505), or Boleslav the Brave (first King of Poland, 1000–1025)—were born into positions of power. Not so El Cid (Rodrigo Díaz de Vivar, lived 1043–1099), the brilliant Spanish general who was said never to have lost a battle. Defeating both Christians and Muslims, he conquered Valencia and ruled it as his own kingdom.

The coronation of France's Louis VIII, one of the great warrior monarchs of the Middle Ages who campaigned to bring the south of France under crown control.

Gerald of Wales describes another successful monarch, Henry II of England (1154–1189):

"Henry II, King of England, had a reddish complexion, rather dark, and a large round head. His eyes were grey, bloodshot, and flashed in anger. He had a fiery countenance.... When his mind was undisturbed, and he was not in an angry mood, he spoke with great eloquence, and what was remarkable in those days, he was well learned."

The High Middle Ages 1000–1300

Crime and Punishment

The most remarkable monarchs not only defended or expanded their realms but also significantly improved the way they were governed. Scotland's David I (1124–1153) was such a ruler. He united his realm, established an ordered society, and imposed a uniform system of law.

Medieval society was used to rough and cruel behavior. To see their will obeyed, therefore, monarchs resorted to the most unpleasant punishments. Henry I of England (1100–1135) was among the most vicious. Furious at the low standard of coins being made (making coins, or minting, was an important royal privilege), at Christmas 1124 he rounded up the manufacturers, castrated them, and cut off their right hands.

Scholars and Saints

A few medieval monarchs, notably Holy Roman Emperor Frederick II, were genuine scholars. England's Henry I's learning earned him the nickname beauclerk (able clerk) and Richard I wrote poetry.

A handful, but not necessarily successful rulers, were made saints after their deaths. They included England's Edward the Confessor (1043–1066), Hungary's Stephen I (1000–1038), Bohemia's prince-duke known as Good King Wenceslas (see panel), and France's Saint Louis. Of saintly queens, one of the more famous was Scotland's Hungarian-born St. Margaret (1069–1093). She was much admired for her civilizing influence over the northern kingdom and for taming her illiterate lunk of a husband, Malcolm Canmore (1058–1093).

St. Wenceslas, remembered in the Christmas carol as a good king, was in fact a martyred duke. He is now the patron saint of the Czech Republic.

Good King Wenceslas (922–927)

Actually a prince-duke rather than a king, Wenceslas learned of Christianity from his grandmother. She was later murdered by his pagan mother. After encouraging German missionaries to come to Bohemia and putting the state under the emperor's protection, he was murdered by his pagan brother, Boleslav.

Royal Failures

KINGSHIP was a dangerous business. Few kings had the talent to rule very well, and a number were failures. As the greatest security came from winning the support of powerful subjects (barons, churchmen, and merchants), so the surest route to failure was to argue with these groups. In the last resort, this might even lead to forcible removal from the throne (deposed).

Battle and Bad Luck

From 1066 to 1500, there were twenty-one monarchs of England. Five, including Edward II (1307–1327), Richard II (1377–1399), Henry VI (1422–1461), Edward V (1483), and Richard III (1483–1485), were deposed; one (William II, 1087–1100) was killed, perhaps deliberately, while hunting; and two, Harold (1066) and Richard I (1189–1199), died as a result of fighting. Almost all of those who died of natural causes had survived serious rebellions at some time or another.

In the end, royal failure could stem from something as straightforward as losing a battle, as happened to Harold.

The Tudors, having seized the crown from the Yorkist Richard III, welcomed propaganda like this by Thomas More:

"Richard the Third ... was ... of small size, with ugly limbs, a crooked back (his left shoulder being much higher than his right), hard faced.... He was close and secret, a deep dissimulater [deceiver], low in appearance, arrogant of heart, outwardly friendly when he inwardly hated, prepared to kiss those he wished to kill...."
The History of King Richard III

Richard II of England surrenders his crown. No English king, however able or ambitious, could afford to ignore the majority of his most powerful subjects.

Charles VI of France (with sword held high) suffers a fit of madness in the forest of Le Mans, 1392. The king's illness left his country open to attack from foreign powers.

Unsuitable

Several monarchs were clearly unsuitable for the task expected of them. Ramiro the Monk of Aragon (1134–1137), for example, was more interested in living an unmarried life devoted to God than in ruling his kingdom. However, when an heir to the throne was needed, he left his monastery, became king, fathered a daughter—then gave up his crown and returned to his monastery.

The greatest tragedy was when a king went insane. This happened to Henry VI of England (1422–1461) and Charles VI of France (1380–1422). Their illnesses led to power struggles and war. England's greatest success during the Hundred Years War was achieved when Charles was insane, and, in turn, England's conquests were then lost when Henry went insane.

Unpopularity was more common than insanity. England's Richard II (1377–1399), Richard III (1483–1485), and Castile's Pedro the Cruel (1349–1369) are examples of monarchs whose harshness led to their downfall. Lack of political skill could have disastrous consequences, too: England's Edward II, tactless and incompetent, was deposed in 1327 and horribly murdered. Such behavior was exceptional. To remove an anointed king, however, was shocking and almost unforgivable.

Killing Kings

Killing a king in battle was just about acceptable—it was an unfortunate fact of life in a warrior society. Thus England's Edward III (1327–1377) was not blamed for the death of John the Blind, King of Bohemia (1311–1346), at the Battle of Crécy; nor Henry VII of England (1485–1509) for the death of Richard III at the Battle of Bosworth. But to murder a king, even if he had given up his kingship, was a crime against God.

Change

MID-ELEVENTH-CENTURY EUROPE was divided into numerous small semi-independent states. Some were kingdoms; the great majority were counties, dukedoms, cities, and other **principalities**. Within many states society was ordered by ties of allegiance and duty, and the authority of the Church was immense. By 1500 much of this early-medieval world had passed away.

Growing Kingdoms

The most obvious change was the way several kingdoms had grown in size during the medieval period, swallowing up lesser neighboring powers (see page 36). England, for example, had absorbed Wales and extended its lordship over Ireland but not Scotland, which had itself expanded in the west at the cost of Norway.

The marriage of Ferdinand of Aragon (1479–1516) and Isabella of Castile (1474–1504) (see page 37) and the conquest of Arab-held southern Spain had united most of the peninsula into a single mighty kingdom. Similarly, by Louis XI's (1461–1483) defeat of Burgundy and the marriage of Charles (1483–1498) with Anne of Brittany (1491), most of modern France was welded into one kingdom.

The power of guns: French forces use cannons to besiege a walled town.

Nationalism

Nationalism is a feeling that binds together people living in a single state and sharing a common culture and language. It emerged during the Middle Ages, often (as in Scotland) in response to an outside threat. People felt they had more in common with those of their own nation, of whatever class, than with those of the same class of another nation. Kings such as England's Henry V (1413–1422) skillfully used nationalist feeling to assist in foreign conquest.

Wealth and Control

The growth in the size of kingdoms was often linked to a rise in monarchical power. Kings of larger kingdoms governed more subjects, although this was more through territorial expansion than population growth: the **Black Death** in the mid-fourteenth century had almost halved Europe's population and recovery had been slow. More recognizable was a general rise in wealth through trade and manufacturing. These factors gave monarchs the potential to raise more from taxation.

The gap between the wealth of the monarchs and their subjects widened. This was particularly obvious in Scotland, where the early Stewart kings' wealth gave them a virtual monopoly of siege cannons. As the Douglas family discovered, this gave monarchs the power to swiftly reduce strongholds of rebellion. Moreover, as the traditional concept of military service to one's lord declined, the monarchs' wealth enabled them to hire larger mercenary armies than potential opponents.

Royal governments were better organized, exerting closer control over difficult individuals and distant regions. The decline in the reputation of the Church also helped monarchical prestige. All these factors, coupled with emerging nationalism, guaranteed monarchy's prominence in the years ahead.

Chepstow Castle, Monmouthshire, Wales, was so well fortified when it was completed in the thirteenth century that it was difficult to take it by force. By the fifteenth century, however, cannons had made such fortresses almost useless in major warfare.

43

Henry VII

THERE ARE SIMILARITIES between the monarchy of the first Norman and the first Tudor: William the Conqueror (1066–1087) and Henry VII (1485–1509). Both came to the throne through military victory in which their predecessors had been killed; both had **papal** support; both faced serious rebellions; both took a close personal interest in government and ruled with handpicked supporters. Nevertheless, remembering that the history of the English monarchy is not one of steady development, the differences between 1066 and 1500 are considerable.

Government

First, Henry VII ruled a single, unified state—England. William's rule had extended over both sides of the English Channel. Second, fifteenth-century government was much more complex and sophisticated than it had been under William I. Henry VII headed a well-tried government machine, which included the council, parliament, law courts, and departments such as the Exchequer, and could entrust his ministers with much of the day-to-day business of government.

In a new move, Henry used a committee of the council known

Renaissance Courts

The Renaissance saw a flourishing of arts, literature, and learning. It began in Italy in the late fourteenth century. It led to monarchs seeking to make their courts magnificent centers of arts and learning. In this respect, Henry VII was far overshadowed by his son, Henry VIII, who lavished money on his court. By Tudor times, the court was becoming the very center of the nation in a way it had almost never been in medieval times.

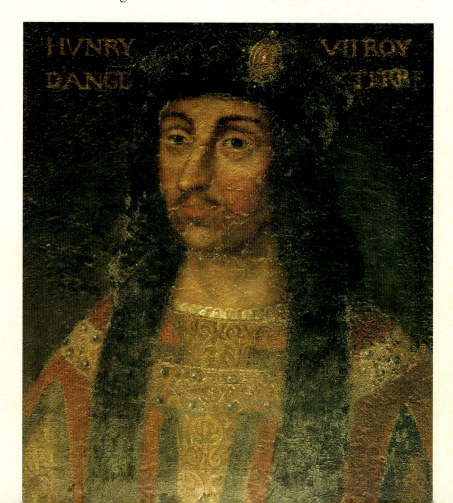

England's Henry VII, founder of the Tudor dynasty, who came to the throne after defeating and slaying Richard III at the Battle of Bosworth, 1485.

The Renaissance court of Henry VIII was clearly distinct in look and manner from those of his medieval predecessors.

as the Council Learned in the Law to hear cases. Whereas the Normans had taken support largely from their family and the barons, the first Tudor relied on those of more humble birth, such as Sir Reynold Bray, Richard Empson, and Edmund Dudley.

The law, always important, played a key role in all aspects of government by Henry's time. Where William I had controlled his barons largely by armed force or the threat of it, Henry used the law. In 1500, forty-six out of England's sixty-two noble families were under the threat of severe legal penalty if they were disloyal.

Court

Henry followed in the footsteps of Richard III and Henry VI by collecting books and supporting learning. The poet John Skelton, for example, was appointed tutor to the young Henry, Duke of York (the future King Henry VIII, 1509–1547).

The majesty in which Henry lived, although not much by European standards, was still a far cry from the uncultured, largely illiterate Norman court. Indeed, at the dawn of the sixteenth century the English monarchy was poised for a splendor and glory undreamed of in the Middle Ages.

The Italian historian Polydore Virgil wrote flatteringly of his English patron, Henry VII:

"In Government he [Henry VII] was shrewd and far-seeing, so that none dared to get the better of him by deceit or sharp practice. He was gracious and kind.... His hospitality was splendidly generous.... He knew well how to maintain his royal dignity and everything belonging to his kingship, at all times and places."

Documents and Debates, Sixteenth Century England 1450–1600

Chronology

800	Pope makes Charlemagne a Roman Emperor.
1034	Emperor Conrad II becomes first Holy Roman Emperor.
1056	Henry IV becomes Holy Roman Emperor.
1066	Death of Edward the Confessor; reign of Harold in England; Battle of Hastings and William I becomes King of England.
1086–1087	*Domesday Book* is compiled.
1087	William II becomes King of England.
1095	Pope Urban II calls for First Crusade.
1100	William II is killed while hunting; Henry I becomes King of England.
1108	Louis VI (the Fat) becomes King of France.
1124	David I becomes King of Scotland.
1137	Eleanor of Aquitaine marries Louis VII of France; Ramiro the Monk abdicates throne of Aragon.
1147–1149	Second Crusade.
1152	Frederick Barbarossa becomes Holy Roman Emperor; Eleanor of Aquitaine marries Henry Plantaganet, the future King of England.
1154	Henry Plantaganet becomes Henry II of England.
1160s	Code of Civil Law of Roman Emperor Justinian is spreading around Europe.
1170	Murder of Thomas Becket.
1180	Philip II (Augustus) becomes King of France.
1189	Richard I (the Lion Heart) becomes King of England. Third Crusade (to 1192).
1199	Richard I dies of wounds; his brother John becomes King of England.
1207	Pope puts England under an interdict.
1212	Frederick II becomes Holy Roman Emperor.
1216	John signs Magna Carta.
1216	John is succeeded by his son Henry III as King of England.
1223	Louis VIII (the Lion) becomes King of France.
1226	Louis IX (Saint Louis) becomes King of France.
1252	Alfonso X becomes King of Castile.
1265	Simon de Montfort summons representatives from counties and towns to meet in a parliament—possibly the beginning of the House of Commons.
1272	Edward I becomes King of England.
1290	First reference to Scottish parliament.
1296	Scottish Wars of Independence begin.
1302	Philip IV of France holds first Estates General.
1306	Robert the Bruce becomes King of Scotland.
1307	Edward II becomes King of England.
1314	Robert the Bruce crushes the English at Bannockburn.
1319	John II becomes King of France.
1327	Edward II of England is dethroned and murdered; Edward III becomes King of England.
1337	Start of Hundred Years War (to 1453).
1346	Edward III of England defeats French at Agincourt.
1356	John II of France captured at Battle of Poitiers.
1358	Peasants' revolt in France.
1369	Pedro the Cruel is removed from the throne of Castile.
1371	Robert Stewart becomes King of Scotland.
1377	Richard II becomes King of England.
1379	Great Schism (to 1417).
1380	Charles VI becomes King of France.
1381	The Peasants' Revolt in England.
1385	Portugal defeats Castile at Aljubarrota.
1399	Richard II of England abdicates and is murdered; Henry IV becomes King of England.
1413	Henry V becomes King of England.
1415	Henry V defeats French at Agincourt.
1422	Death of Henry V, Henry VI becomes King of England; Charles VII (The Victorious) becomes King of France.
1431	Joan of Arc martyred in France.
1450	Wars of Roses begin in England.
1453	Calais is the only English possession remaining in France.
1460	Scotland's James II is blown up by his own cannon.
1461	Henry VI is replaced by Edward IV; Louis XI becomes King of France.
1469	Marriage of Ferdinand of Aragon and Isabella of Castile.
1471	Queen Margaret is imprisoned in the Tower of London.
1472	Ivan the Great of Russia becomes the Tsar.
1483	Death of Edward IV of England; murder of Edward V of England by Richard III who becomes King of England.
1485	Richard III is slain at Bosworth; Henry VII becomes the first Tudor king in England.
1487	Battle of Stoke ends the Wars of the Roses.
1488	James IV becomes King of Scotland.
1509	Henry VIII becomes King of England.

Glossary

Anglo Saxon   Relating to the two groups of Germanic peoples, the Angles and the Saxons, who settled in Britain from the fifth century onward.

baron   Medieval nobleman.

Black Death   Killer disease, also known as the bubonic plague, which produces dark swellings on its victims.

chancery   The department of the English Lord Chancellor. Originally responsible for secretarial business, it later concentrated on legal matters.

chivalry   Code of honor and behavior of a knight.

Christendom   Christians worldwide, who are regarded as one body.

clergy   Men and women who work in the Church as priests, monks, and nuns, for example.

common land   Land open to everyone to use.

common people   Another term for the Third Estate.

coronation   The ceremony at which a new monarch is crowned.

courtier   A person who regularly attends the royal court.

crusade   The attempt by Christian warriors to capture holy sites, such as Jerusalem, from the Muslims.

duke   The highest inherited title of the noble classes.

excommunicate   Cut off from the Church.

hereditary   The passing on of possessions, characteristics, or titles (as in the nobility) through the family, particularly from one generation to the next.

Holy Roman Emperor   Honorary title given to a powerful German ruler.

housecarls   Anglo Saxon monarch's professional bodyguards.

interdict   A measure banning all Church activity, including burials and marriages.

justice   Someone who hands down the law in a court.

mercenary   Soldier who fights for money, often in foreign lands.

nationalism   Loyalty to one's nation.

nobility   A group of people belonging by rank, title, or birth to the aristocracy.

officers of state   Important royal servants, or ministers.

papal   Of, or relating to, the pope.

peasants' revolt/The Peasants' Revolt   Rebellion of lower classes against the ruling classes.

pike   Infantry spear used to defend against cavalry attack.

pilgrim   A person who journeys to a sacred place for religious purposes.

principality   A region run by a prince but also used to mean any state or country under a single government.

prior   A priest with responsibilities over monks.

ransom   Money paid for the return of a captured warrior.

regent   A person who rules in place of a monarch that is too old or too ill to rule.

scrofula   A skin disease, possibly a form of tuberculosis.

secular   Not spiritual or sacred.

siege engine   Machine for bombarding a castle.

subject   A person under the rule of a monarch.

succession   Following someone to, or inheriting, the crown.

Third Estate   Ordinary people, i.e., those who are neither clergy nor nobility.

vassal   Someone who swears allegiance to a lord.

For Further Research

J.J. Bagley and P.B. Rowley, eds., *A Documentary History of England*. Harmondsworth, UK: Pelican, 1966.

Norman F. Cantor, ed., *The Medieval World: 300-1300*. New York: Macmillan, 1963.

Denys Cook, ed., *Documents and Debates: Sixteenth Century England 1450–1600*. New York: Macmillan, 1980.

Jean Baptiste Duriselle, *Europe: A History of Its Peoples*. Trans. Richard Maynes. London: Viking, 1990.

G.R. Elton, ed., *Renaissance and Reformation 1300–1648*. New York: Macmillan, 1963.

G.N. Garmonsway, trans., *The Anglo Saxon Chronicle*. London: Dent/Everyman 2nd edition, 1972.

Elizabeth Hallam, ed., *Chronicles of the Crusades*. London: Weidenfeld & Nicholson, 1989.

Bryce Lyon, ed., *The High Middle Ages 1000–1300*. New York: Macmillan, 1964.

Index